FIVE SMOOTH STONES

Learning to overcome our Goliaths

Richard C. George

short course

resources@thewayofthespirit.com
www.thewayofthespirit.com

First published in Great Britain in 2006
by The Way of the Spirit,
Framingham Earl Hall, Framingham Earl, Norwich,
Norfolk NR14 7SB
Registered Charity No. 1110648

2nd Edition published in 2011
Reprinted 2013

3rd Edition published in 2015

Copyright © 2011 Richard C. George

All rights reserved. No part of this publication may be reproduced, stored in a retrieval system, or transmitted, in any form or by any means, electronic, mechanical, photocopying, recording or otherwise, without the permission, in writing, of the publisher.

ISBN 978-1-9085-2800-1

Scripture taken from the
HOLY BIBLE, NEW INTERNATIONAL VERSION.
Copyright © 1973, 1978, 1984 by International Bible Society. Used by permission of Hodder and Stoughton Limited.

Bible Reading Course

The purpose of this booklet and the CD that goes with it is partly to give you some impression of how The Way of the Spirit Bible Reading Course works. It is not, however, just an excerpt or collection of excerpts from the fuller course, but a properly integrated short course in its own right, and as such is somewhat different in presentation.

- The full course takes you systematically through the whole Bible, chapter by chapter, with the help of a textbook; here you have only a little booklet giving a brief survey of a Bible theme.
- The full course has more comprehensive worksheets.
- The course CDs offer more systematic teaching arranged in twenty-minute parts (the CD accompanying this booklet contains one continuous talk).

Nevertheless, by using these materials you should capture the flavour of the full course quite well. The purpose of The Way of the Spirit is to teach about the aliveness of the Bible and the power of the Spirit revealed in its pages, to help you understand what the Bible is all about, what the way of God's Spirit is in it, and how to enter more fully into the richness of life men of Bible-times enjoyed. You should find all these aims met in some measure as you use Five Smooth Stones.

May God bless you richly as you study His Word.

How to Use This Booklet

It is arranged in two parts:

- The first (pages 7-35) introduces the study.
- The second (pages 36-52) is a four-part question sheet.

A single teaching CD with a talk to accompany the booklet is also available. (To obtain this, please write to The Way of the Spirit or visit our website.)

You can use this booklet in several different ways:

- By itself with your Bible.
- Along with the CD and your Bible.
- By studying in a group.

Whichever method you choose, learn to listen for what the Holy Spirit has to tell you—about your beliefs, attitudes and life-style. Ask yourself what lessons you should be learning from your readings, so that you can apply them to your own understanding and life as a Christian.

Part Two, the study guide, has introductory notes on page 36 with further suggestions about how to use it. Each part of this section has questions that will help you determine what you have learned and encourage you to apply that in practical living. The notes have been prepared in such a way that you can use them privately or in a group. Experience has shown that group study is much more fruitful.

If you use the CD, you may find it helpful to listen to the relevant part before starting your readings. If you do this, you should also listen to it again afterwards. Not all the answers to the questions will be found in the booklet—this is intentional!

If you use this booklet in a group you will need to listen to the CD in your meeting. Then discuss your answers to the questions, share your insights and encourage one another to grow in the Lord. Remember to allow time for prayer and fellowship as well.

Preface to Second Edition

Near the beginning of the text book **My Lord and my God**[1] John McKay lists some who encouraged him in his journey of faith. *But, he says, it is in ministry that the value of faith and revelation is discovered. Over the last eight years the truths the Spirit has shown me have been well tested and the teachings of earlier years thoroughly sifted.*[2]

I understand this much more today than I did eleven years ago when I stepped out for myself in 'ministry'. It's not so much the ministry itself which is the tutor (sometimes it feels as though the ministry itself is the easiest bit!) but all those challenges which accompany it and are around it - this is where the testing and sifting that John speaks of happens! It is a small selection of such challenges I faced at different times that form the basis of this study. I've been encouraged by the anecdotal evidence I've received from others who have been helped by hearing what I learned along the way. It seems these things were not peculiar to me but were things many have also struggled with!

James, in his New Testament letter, insists that we consider our trials joyful. I can't say I've mastered that one yet, though there is great joy in discovering

---

[1] McKay, J. My Lord and my God Kingdom Faith, 1990 Available from www.thewayoftthespirit.com
[2] Pg xiii-xiv

answers in the bible and in finding the Holy Spirit not only illuminating the words, but also sending the power and grace to live them out. How many have discovered a previously unknown Psalm speaking directly into their specific and personal circumstances - usually when they're on their knees crying out to God for some breakthrough in a desperate place? Isn't it wonderful when we finally learn that our answers are not to be found in man's knowledge! Rather, it is in God's own wisdom - mysteriously revealed only as we look for it as for silver and search for it as for hidden treasure[3], that we find what we need. The fear of the Lord is indeed the beginning of wisdom.

I, too, thank God for those who have taught me to love and treasure the Bible, to believe it and to want to live by it. In days where there are so many alternative places to look - each intriguing and beguiling in its own way – many long for a return to the word and the Spirit in the church (let alone outside it!).

As with every The Way of the Spirit short course **Five Smooth Stones** is best done as a Bible study, using the study sections at the end to guide discussion and thought. It is no great literary work! Its aim is to guide the reader into closer walk with God through a greater love for the Bible.

There are some changes to the manuscript in this second edition, mainly grammatical and for clarity,

---

[3] Proverbs 2.4

though I've added some further explanation to the third 'stone', which may help understand it better but which certainly doesn't change the substance of what was outlined in the first edition. Perhaps the main addition is in the prayer, which I've included at the end after the study section to help those who need to find words to summarise what they've just discovered.

RCG April 2011, Norwich

1.

FIVE SMOOTH STONES PART ONE

CALLED TO OVERCOME

We are called to be overcomers: those who rise above the storms of life and testings of faith.

So David triumphed over the Philistines with a sling and a stone. (1 Samuel 17:50)

As he called David to defeat Goliath, God calls us to fight and win certain battles. It is out of the cauldron of difficulty, opposition and struggle in our lives that the weapons we fight with are forged, and this is as true today in a post-modern, 'post-Christian' world as ever throughout the history of Christendom.

We are called to be overcomers (see, for instance, the ending of each of Christ's letters to the churches in Revelation chapters 2 & 3): those who rise above the storms of life and testings of faith, using them to bring forth something fruitful and holy in our lives. Rather

FIVE SMOOTH STONES
Learning to overcome our Goliaths

than running away from our Goliaths we are to face them with the same spirit David had, even to be led willingly into such battles. We are to trust God always to bring us through, believing his promises in every testing situation, tenaciously moving forwards and proclaiming as Job did, 'When I've been tested I shall come forth as gold!'

God's sovereignty

To know God as sovereign is to understand that He ultimately rules over every situation in our lives.

For us to overcome as the battle rages, we need to know that God is truly sovereign - for if he is not, we have little foundation on which to stand. Job encountered God in his sovereignty and exclaimed 'My ears had heard of you, but now my eyes have seen you.' (Job 42:5) Job had been a religious man all his life, indeed he is described as blameless and upright (Job 1:1) yet meeting God in this way changed everything and he overcame his trial without ever needing to understand why God had allowed it.

To know God as sovereign is to understand that He ultimately rules over every situation in our lives, even over the lives of people around us – whether they know him or not. (A good biblical example is when he chose to use King Cyrus of Persia, a gentile, to free the Israelites from captivity in Babylon.) To know him as sovereign is to know that just as he restored everything in Job's life (and as he used Cyrus), so he is able to override our circumstances, and influence others. It is to know that there is no situation that is beyond his sphere of influence.

FIVE SMOOTH STONES
Learning to overcome our Goliaths

Earlier, when Israel was being marched off to exile in Babylon, God spoke to them of this sovereignty through the prophet Isaiah:

Do you not know? Have you not heard? Has it not been told you from the beginning? Have you not understood since the earth was founded? He sits enthroned above the circle of the earth, and its people are like grasshoppers. He stretches out the heavens like a canopy, and spreads them out like a tent to live in. He brings princes to naught, and reduces the rulers of this world to nothing...to whom will you compare me? Or who is my equal? says the Holy One. Lift up your eyes and look to the heavens. Who created all these? He who brings out the starry host one by one, and calls them each by name...do you not know? Have you not heard? The Lord is the everlasting God, the creator of the ends of the earth. (Isaiah 40:21-28)

In these exciting middle chapters of Isaiah (40-55) he lifts the eyes of Israel, revealing himself in new ways as the one who is over all things. 'Don't you know, Israel, that your God is the one who created everything? You're concerned about having been thrown out of the land I promised your forefathers, and you think the adventure's over, but look again at whom I truly am — no one can thwart me! Don't you see — it's only just begun!'

Later he tells them that he is even sovereign over 'the destroyer' too, for Satan is merely a created being, a creature:

FIVE SMOOTH STONES
Learning to overcome our Goliaths

See it is I who created the blacksmith who fans the coals into flame and forges a weapon fit for its work. And it is I who have created the destroyer to work havoc; no weapon forged against you will prevail, and you will refute every tongue that accuses you. (Isaiah 54:16-17).

Some might imagine that there is a war going on in the heavens between two opposing forces, and the outcome hangs in the balance. This is not, nor has it ever been, the case. God created everything, including Satan, so a creature is all he is. *Do you not know, have you not heard, the Lord is the everlasting God, the creator of the ends of the earth!*

Christ in his humanity walked in full confidence that his Father in heaven is over all and faithful to all he had promised. It is this trust in his sovereignty that is so often tested, a trust which he nevertheless insists on working into us as we learn to walk with him.

Change them Lord!

> *Our battles are internal; they go on in our own hearts and reveal, very often, our own rebellion, worldliness and unbelief.*

Very often we want God to be sovereign over that other person's life more than our own! We'd like him to reign over and to change them. It's important to know that he can; yet, frustratingly, it appears that very often it's not that other person God wants to change, it's us. Our battles are internal; they go on in our own hearts and reveal, very often, our own rebellion, worldliness and unbelief. God calls each of us to fight and win these battles, to see his kingdom expand in our own hearts and lives.

FIVE SMOOTH STONES
Learning to overcome our Goliaths

Even our struggles to resist demonic forces in our lives very often boil down to a single issue: do we believe what his word tells us about the authority we have in Christ over Satan? It's not a life or death struggle against some spiritual force in a spiritual realm — it's a matter of what's going on in our heart; do we believe Satan is simply another creature, one whom Jesus has defeated on the cross? If so, it becomes a simple matter of faith to refuse to give him a foothold, and to resist and stand firm against him, knowing that he must flee[4].

It's our heart that is the real issue; and with an attitude like David's we can learn to overcome. As we do so we are changed more and more into the likeness of Christ.

Of course our heart is tested most when we are moving forwards in his kingdom purposes. Should we stand still in our Christian life then there is less pressure on us and less reason to reach out for still deeper revelation of God's sovereignty and faithfulness. Conversely when we desire to bear more fruit for him the battle intensifies.

David prepares for the fight

It's our heart that is the real issue.

David spent his early years tending sheep. Out there in the meadows he learned to protect his flock from marauding wild animals. With no one watching him, he practised his weapons, learning to fight off every

---

[4] We do have to do this, for he is real and does oppose us from time to time; but we do not have to go overboard, making our demonology more dominant than our Christology.

FIVE SMOOTH STONES
Learning to overcome our Goliaths

potential threat to his sheep. When he finally got his chance to destroy Goliath he told Saul:

Your servant has been keeping his father's sheep. When a lion or bear came and carried off a sheep from the flock, I went after it, struck it and rescued the sheep from its mouth. When it turned on me, I seized it by its hair, struck it and killed it. Your servant has killed both the lion and the bear; this uncircumcised Philistine will be like one of them, because he has defied the armies of the living God. (1 Samuel 17:34-36)

Then, while others cowered in fear of the taunting giant, he showed the same fighting attitude as he had had towards the wild animals. Just as he went after lions and bears in the meadows, so he went after Goliath using five smooth stones he'd collected from the stream (1 Samuel 17:40). Using his sling, one of these stones scored a direct hit and Goliath fell to the ground, dead.

David had turned down the armour offered to him by Saul and chose to fight with the weapons he'd become familiar with during the years spent shepherding. No doubt he'd spent many solitary hours practising his aim, until he knew he could take a stone and hit his target with certainty. When the time came to fight Goliath he chose not to put on the armour of a traditional soldier but to rely on the weapons God had taught him to use — that with which he was familiar and confident. For God knew what he would need!

FIVE SMOOTH STONES
Learning to overcome our Goliaths

Human hearts

> *Confident in Christ's victory on the cross, we can face our own weakness, vulnerability and fear.*

What in the Old Testament are presented in terms of real battles between warring factions, become in the New Testament battles in (not between!) human hearts. They are no less dramatic, significant or exhilarating; they are just as crucial and dangerous — and we can take up arms with the confidence of knowing that Jesus has already won the battle for us.

Confident in Christ's victory on the cross, we can face our own weakness, vulnerability and fear. Much of the time our biggest problem is lack of faith: not truly believing what Christ has done, who he is and who we now are in him. Making progress in our walk with God is inevitably bloody and messy at times. Avoiding the bloodiness and mess in the name of religion or 'righteousness' is to avoid the very battles Jesus has called us to fight and win.

We have opportunities daily to practise our weapons. Just as David learned to use the sling in everyday skirmishes with wild animals, and in so doing became an expert, so the circumstances and people God allows in our lives are there for us to learn how to handle our 'weapons' and to win battles. It is not the circumstances or other people that God intends to change - it's us!

Then, once the battle in our hearts is won, *we can change the circumstances around us.*

FIVE SMOOTH STONES
Learning to overcome our Goliaths

Just as David took the stones and mastered how to sling them, so we can take the weapon God gives us (from his word), master it and use it effectively to change our hearts and extend his kingdom. He gives us plenty of practice 'in the meadows', speaking through his word by his Spirit, thereby training us in the secret (and sometimes not so secret!) place.

Each stone is the word brought alive by the Holy Spirit. The invitation accompanying each revelation is to take it, process it and learn to use it. Slowly but surely, in the Holy Spirit's school, the revelation becomes reality.

And we know that in all things God works for the good of those who love him, who have been called according to his purpose. (Romans 8:28)

Once we have yielded our lives to the kingship of Christ (so that he is our Lord and not just our saviour), he will use every circumstance and person and situation for our good, turning every difficult circumstance and relationship into an opportunity to become more like him. The truths he teaches us during these are times like the stones David learned to use in his sling.

When we walk choosing to face the Goliaths in our heart we are forced to cry out to God. Overcoming seems impossible, yet he watches over us as we stumble around, and as we keep our eyes on him, we learn how to handle these impossible situations. Eventually, wanting to bear fruit for him and become like Christ, we learn to pick for ourselves the right stones from the stream. Christ bursts forth in our lives.

FIVE SMOOTH STONES
Learning to overcome our Goliaths

They become weapons of Christlikeness in a fallen world.

Grasping this, we change the way we see our lives, circumstances and those around us. We will cease projecting our sin onto others in an effort to avoid facing our own sinfulness, unbelief, and fear. It is to see everything that happens to us as an opportunity to grow more like him.

Five smooth stones

> *He sees the end from the beginning and has a purpose for each of our lives.*

God knows the stones he wants us to learn to handle. He sees the end from the beginning and has a purpose for each of our lives. The stones won't change just because we reject them! They're ours to take, polish, master and eventually treasure. They are invariably not ones we'd pick for ourselves, to have resting comfortably in our shepherd's pouch. They're the ones that we find most difficult and cost the most (the death of our flesh!) The pain is predominantly in these early stages though, and as we continue fighting they become our most effective weapons, just as they did for David.

Here are some stones God is teaching me to use. I'm still polishing and taking aim, and I'm even learning to treasure them. They are definitely a 'work in progress'. They relate, I imagine, to how we all protect our hearts when under pressure from those around us. These five stones overlap and interconnect. I need them all.

There's one image I carry that encapsulates what God is attempting to work in my heart. That is of Jesus, as he is

FIVE SMOOTH STONES
Learning to overcome our Goliaths

presented to the crowd by Pilate. It is described in John 19, and although it doesn't say so, for some reason I always imagine that Jesus walks out onto a balcony. (Maybe I saw that on some old film once!)

Jesus and Pilate

He is full of the father's love for all mankind.

Then Pilate took Jesus and had him flogged. The solders twisted together a crown of thorns and put it on his head. They clothed him in a purple robe and went up to him again, saying 'Hail king of the Jews!' and they struck him in the face. Once more Pilate came out and said to the Jews 'Look, I'm bringing him out to let you know that I find no basis of a charge against him.' When Jesus came out wearing the crown of thorns and the purple robe, Pilate said to them 'Here is the man!' (John 19:1-5)

Here is Jesus, in his humanity, by now understanding who he is, what he is here for and what lies ahead of him. He is going to the cross, and his aim is the restoration of all creation, including the jeering crowd and soldiers beating and mocking him. He is full of the father's love for all mankind, even this crowd, and is about to die a horrible death for them. The gospel account doesn't show us how he looked at them: the expression on his face, or how he walked out. I imagine him coming out with dignity and with love in his eyes, with no trace of anger, resentment or bitterness. Instead he is full of love and compassion, even for those beating him up.

He was oppressed and afflicted yet he did not open his mouth; he was led like a lamb to the slaughter and as a

FIVE SMOOTH STONES
Learning to overcome our Goliaths

sheep before her shearers is silent, so he did not open his mouth.' (Isaiah 53:7)

In Acts, there is a description of Stephen's face under similar circumstances. We read that he 'had the face of an angel' as he preached to the Sanhedrin before they stoned him to death. After he had spoken, they were furious and gnashed their teeth at him. But, full of the Holy Spirit, Stephen looked up to heaven and saw the son of man standing there. While they were stoning him, he cried out, just as Jesus had on the cross, *Lord, do not hold this sin against them.* (Acts 7:60)

The grace of God can provide us this 'dignity of Christ' at any time. Many Christian martyrs over the centuries have known such grace in their moments of trial and we can reach out for it in our own too. Yet it is more commonly in the daily trials of life that God shows us our need, and in the school of the Holy Spirit there is not always a quick and easy route to things that he wants us to master in our own hearts. I have found myself wondering sometimes whether the life of a martyr is the easier option: one death and it's all over, whereas most of us are called to carry our crosses every day!

FIVE SMOOTH STONES
Learning to overcome our Goliaths

First STONE: A NEW HEART

Jesus the king had come with the kingdom, and the miracles were signs of the breaking-in of that kingdom.

I will give you a new heart and put a new spirit in you. (Ezekiel 36:26)

Above all else guard your heart, for it is the wellspring of life. (Proverbs 4.23)

The Pharisees came up from Jerusalem to spy on Jesus (Mark 7). They found his disciples disobeying the strict Jewish code then in force – they found them eating food with hands that were unwashed. This account happens soon after – and despite - Jesus miraculously feeding the 5,000 then stilling the storm after walking to the disciples on the lake. Chapter 6 ends and all who touched him were healed. Jesus the king had come with the kingdom, and the miracles were signs of the breaking-in of that kingdom. It would replace the legalistic system of religious activity that had developed and hardened since the Jews had returned from captivity 400 years earlier. He had come to bring life — life in all its fullness[5].

In spite of the manifest evidence of this kingdom life, the Pharisees remained critical and nit picking. Jesus denounced them as hypocrites, as those who had *let go of the commands of God and (held) on to the traditions of men* (7:8). He then told them that their external

---

[5] See the short course *Water to Wine* in this same series for a study from John's Gospel on what Jesus came to bring.

FIVE SMOOTH STONES
Learning to overcome our Goliaths

religious things counted for nothing, for it was a man's heart that mattered: *Don't you see that nothing that enters a man from the outside can make him 'unclean', for it doesn't go into his heart but into his stomach...it's what comes out of a man's heart that makes him unclean* (paraphrased Mark 7.18)[6].

In the next scene (Mark 7.24-30), as if to underline Jesus' teaching about the heart, true faith is shown by a Greek (and presumably) gentile woman. She fell at Jesus' feet and asked for healing for her daughter. Jesus is moved by her faith, which was in stark contrast to the legalistic attitudes of the Pharisees, and he duly delivers her daughter of the demons. But it is Jesus' earlier comments to the Pharisees that are of most interest to us here.

Nothing outside a man can make him unclean!

It is not the things outside us that create problems.

The statement Jesus makes to the Pharisees is the gateway to personal breakthrough in so many of those relationships and circumstances we struggle with. For it is not the things outside us that create problems, the problem is only ever in our heart. It is not the circumstances or that other person that is the problem; it is how we have responded to them. As one great

---

[6] This wasn't a new concept! When choosing the next king from among Jesse's sons, God had told Samuel, *the Lord does not look at the things man looks at. Man looks at the outward appearance but God looks at the heart.* (1 Samuel 16.7) What Jesus had come to do was far more radical than to change merely external things – he was coming to make men's hearts acceptable to God

FIVE SMOOTH STONES
Learning to overcome our Goliaths

preacher used to say, relationships don't cause problems, they just expose them!

There is nothing *out there* that can prevent me from walking in the good of all that Christ won for me on the cross – the new heart that he has given me! He died that I might be free, free from resentment, bitterness, envy and strife in my relationships, and *no person or circumstance can rob me of that freedom unless I let them*. The important question is: what's going on in my heart?

Paul wrote some of his best letters from prison. So did Dietrich Bonhoeffer. John Bunyan wrote Pilgrim's Progress under lock and key. They may have been in prison but in their hearts they remained free. People can take away many things from me, including my freedom, but they cannot take away the new heart that is mine in Christ.

What will rob me, and imprison me, is my wrong response to what happens around me, particularly any wrong responses to other people. *Above all else guard your heart, for it is the wellspring of life* (Proverbs 4.23).

Nothing outside a man can make him unclean; it is only that which comes from his heart! How did Jesus stand with such dignity before Pilate and the crowd? He protected his heart, not allowing negativity or wrong thinking to break into his heart of love; and with a conquering spirit like David's we can do the same. God has given us a new heart and we are responsible for it. Nothing external can harm us — unless we let it.

FIVE SMOOTH STONES
Learning to overcome our Goliaths

Second Stone: Who Controls Me

> *We used to be stuck with the flesh; now we're born again of the Spirit we can choose to walk in the Spirit.*

You however, are not controlled by the flesh, but by the Spirit... (Romans 8.9a)

Chapter 8 is the great climax to Paul's letter to the Romans. In it he talks of life in the Spirit and of walking in the Spirit. In v. 5-8 the mind of one set on what the Holy Spirit desires is contrasted with one that is led by the flesh. Verse 9 reads: *You however are not controlled by the flesh, but by the Spirit.* We all know of course that we are more than capable, even though the Holy Spirit lives in us, of acting according to our own flesh! Paul's point is, we now have a choice! We can walk in the spirit, or in the flesh. We used to be stuck with the flesh; now we're born again of the Spirit we can choose to walk in the Spirit; to be led by the Spirit.

The Good News

In other words, now that I am a child of God, I can be led by the Spirit which enables me to walk like Christ did — it enables me to bear the fruit of the Holy Spirit: love, joy, peace patience, kindness, goodness, faithfulness and self-control. I can do that because the Holy Spirit is in me, not because it's natural to me. This can be a reality in my life because Christ died and gave me a new heart, one like his, and poured his Spirit into me. I am no longer bound by my natural responses — governed as they so often were by fear, pride and self-

FIVE SMOOTH STONES
Learning to overcome our Goliaths

protection, but I can choose to live in the reality of Christ in me instead.

This is good news! I am not locked into the self-destructive behaviour patterns of my flesh — the part of me that rebels against the Lordship of Christ in my life. Jesus has saved me from that. I can choose instead to draw upon his Holy Spirit within me. I can practise drawing upon Christ-in-me until it becomes natural for me to be led by the Spirit, even under pressure.

It's even better news when you consider that the word 'flesh' in the verse doesn't just refer to your own flesh but to everyone else's too. So my 'amplified' version (!) would read: *You however are not controlled by the flesh* **(mine or anyone else's)** *but by the Spirit.*[7]

I need never again react to anybody else's flesh, however intimidating or controlling it may seem. Whatever comes from the flesh need never *make* me react in any other way than in line with the fruit of the Holy Spirit in me (Christ-in-me). This will take some practise, but is entirely possible because the Holy Spirit lives in me. I can choose how I respond. I *can* choose!! Remember —nothing outside me makes me unclean, only that which comes from my heart. The other person's flesh cannot make me unclean, it is only my reaction to him that will serve to do that.

It helped me enormously when I understood that even God doesn't control people (he could but he doesn't!),

---

[7] **Words in brackets are my addition**

FIVE SMOOTH STONES
Learning to overcome our Goliaths

and if he doesn't, who are we to? I am not to control anyone else, nor are they to control me. There is only one person in the whole universe I can control, and that's myself. And I have all the resources of heaven within me to enable me to do so. I am in control of my responses and reactions.

This is not due to great self-effort of course; I may have tried that all my life and failed miserably. It's because God lives in me, and so by faith he produces the fruit of self-control in my life which then come forth rather than my own fallen reactions. As I choose to look at him, rather than the circumstances and how I feel about them, he then leads me into freedom from the flesh – mine or anyone else's.

THIRD STONE: WISDOM FROM HEAVEN

> *It is only wisdom from heaven that we should be listening to.*

But the wisdom that comes from heaven is first of all pure, then peace-loving, considerate, submissive, full of mercy and good fruit, impartial and sincere. (James 3.14-18)

It might happen that someone says something to me that I'm not sure is from the flesh or from the Spirit. What should I do with it? I tend to err on the side of listening anyway — in case there's something in it that's from the Lord, and I therefore should be taking note of it. But this isn't always a helpful thing to do! It is only wisdom from heaven that we should be listening

FIVE SMOOTH STONES
Learning to overcome our Goliaths

to — and if it isn't from God then we may need to protect ourselves from it.

Discerning whether we allow words spoken to us to influence us is vital. As we seek to walk by the light of God's word to us, allowing it to be a lamp unto our path, we need to know what he is saying and where he is leading! As we decide to live our lives unto God, walking the path he alone lays out before us, we need to hear his words to us and know when to shun anything else. Our own reason cannot do it, nor can any good intention to listen to everybody that has an opinion. Jesus knew *what was in the heart of a man* and we must too!

There's an even more important reason not to listen to wrong things than needing to know where God is leading us: to protect our hearts. I was watching an animated version of Lord of the Rings a little while ago. There was a scene where Frodo had been injured in a fight, and was being carried on a stretcher by his friends. Sam, his closest friend, asked Aragorn as they walked along what had happened to Frodo. He replied something like, 'He was wounded by a sword. The tip broke off and made its way towards his heart. If it had reached his heart he would have died.' This is exactly what happens to us. We are wounded by the words of others (their flesh), and if we allow the wrong things to penetrate and reach our heart they can damage and even be fatal to our spiritual lives. *Above all else guard your heart for it is the wellspring of life.*

FIVE SMOOTH STONES
Learning to overcome our Goliaths

Satan loves to attack us with his words and thoughts (sometimes through the mouths of others — maybe even those close to us) and wants those words to travel towards, and ultimately reach our hearts — the new hearts that Christ died to give us, the wellspring of life from which rivers of the living water should flow, bringing the life of Christ and victory over all darkness and deadness. Yet hearts tainted by resentment, unforgiveness, bitterness and negativity cannot also be the source of streams of living water. It is easier not to let these things near our hearts than to get rid of them once they are.

James shows us how we might begin to discern the difference between that which may be from God, and is therefore always worth listening to, and that which is not from God and should not be entertained: *But if you harbour bitter envy and selfish ambition in your hearts, do not boast about it or deny the truth. Such 'wisdom' does not come down from heaven but is earthly, unspiritual, of the devil. For where you have envy and selfish ambition, there you find disorder and every evil practice. But the wisdom that comes from heaven is first of all pure; then peace loving, considerate, submissive, full of mercy and good fruit, impartial and sincere. Peacemakers who sow in peace raise a harvest of righteousness.* (James 3:14-18)

The bit to concentrate on is in the second half of the passage about wisdom from heaven. If the words are from God — and contain something I need to hear — then they will come from a heart that is *peace loving,*

FIVE SMOOTH STONES
Learning to overcome our Goliaths

submissive, full of mercy and good fruit, impartial and sincere. So I need to take good note of what's said, however much I may not want to! But if the words come more from some other sort of heart, maybe even one more resembling more as described in the first half of the passage, from a root of envy or ambition, then I may decide that I should not allow the words anywhere near my heart. I need to protect it against ungodly 'wisdom', that which can cause damage. Sometimes that means not even listening, but walking away.

FOURTH STONE: FORGIVENESS

Forgive, as the Lord forgave you. (Colossians 3.13)

> *I have been forgiven everything, so who am I to carry anything against another — for whom Christ also died?*

Here's my fourth stone, and it is entwined with the first three. It's forgiveness: the bottom line written in our hearts from which our attitudes towards others grow and remain healthy.

Christ died that we might be forgiven. Who then are we to hold anything against each other? Forgiveness was won for us on the cross. I have been forgiven everything, so who am I to carry anything against another — for whom Christ also died? If Jesus forgives them, how can we not? Yet it is not automatic that I walk in forgiveness. R.T. Kendall wrote a book called Total Forgiveness and concluded that walking in forgiveness every day was *the* most difficult thing in the Christian life. Nor was this an ancient truth for him; even after years of high profile ministry he had learned

FIVE SMOOTH STONES
Learning to overcome our Goliaths

it relatively recently, as God had showed him that he was walking in unforgiveness in a certain situation that had caused him hurt.

We cannot forgive as God asks us to without his grace. A year or two ago, I went to bed one night feeling resentful towards Sarah, my wife. (The issue is unimportant — I can't even recall it now, it was probably something really small that I had taken offence about, and which was no doubt my fault anyway!). As I lay there trying to get to sleep I knew I had to let the offence go. Yet I also knew I didn't feel able. I cried out for his grace as I fell asleep, feeling defeated. I awoke as usual early the next morning and went downstairs for my time with God. I began praying and was immediately aware again of my inability to forgive. I cried out to God and did the only thing I could think to do: praise him and focus on who he was and what he had done for me. As I did this, I was aware of the Holy Spirit filling me afresh. I had a great sense of his Spirit upon me and in a moment every negative attitude, thought and feeling lifted. Rather than creep up to Sarah a little later with defeat and heaviness in my heart I bounded up the stairs with a cup of tea for her in my hand and gave her a big hug! I was free! Not by my self-effort, but by the grace of God.

Grace is what we need, each day. None of these 'stones' are, in the final analysis, things we achieve by trying harder. They are truths to receive by faith, and to walk in with determination. This comes only through revelation of freedom we have in Christ. It requires a

FIVE SMOOTH STONES
Learning to overcome our Goliaths

determination to live in the good of what Christ has done for us. It was so easy to forgive others when we first got saved — it takes a certain attitude to live in his grace all the time. These things do not depend upon our feelings; they rely on the truth of what Jesus did on the cross.

In the evening of that first day of the week, when the disciples were together, with the doors locked for fear of the Jews, Jesus came and stood among them and said, 'Peace be with you!' After he had said this, he showed them his hands and side. The disciples were overjoyed when they saw the Lord. Again Jesus said, 'Peace be with you! As the father has sent me, I am sending you.' And with that he breathed on them and said, 'Receive the Holy Spirit. If you forgive anyone his sins, they are forgiven; if you do not forgive them, they are not forgiven.' (John 20:19-23)

This is an astonishing passage. In the wider context — from Chapter 19:41 onwards — John is comparing the day of the resurrection of Jesus with the first day of creation. Both happen 'on the first day of the week' and the events of each are set in a garden. In Genesis God breathes his life into Adam and here Jesus breathes his life, the Holy Spirit, upon the disciples. It is the start of a new day! The resurrection of Jesus is comparable to the event of creation itself. John is describing a re-creation and as such it is an important event in the history of everything. The first thing Jesus commands his disciples, having breathed his Spirit on them, is to forgive others — actually it's more than a command, he

FIVE SMOOTH STONES
Learning to overcome our Goliaths

gives them his authority to forgive on his behalf. Forgiveness is so important in the eternal plan of re-creation that it is the first thing Jesus wants the disciples to understand. You must forgive!! It's as though he is saying, *my whole plan depended on forgiving you, and now — restored — you must live in the good of what I have done, and forgive others yourself!*

If we aspire to be spiritual, to see miracles, the deeper things of the kingdom, to walk in the higher purposes of God we must first of all learn — in the power of the Holy Spirit — to forgive: the world, each other and ourselves.

FIFTH STONE: THE JUDGE WAS JUDGED!

In place of judgement he would bring forgiveness of sin and empowerment by the Holy Spirit.

Humble yourselves, therefore, under God's mighty hand, that he may lift you up in due time. (1 Peter 6)

When the Old Testament prophets looked ahead to the 'day of the Lord' it was often to a day of fire when God would come and judge mankind. The day of the Lord was, for some prophets, the day of reckoning, when God would come and restore the kingdom to Israel. Others more optimistically looked ahead to the outpouring of the Holy Spirit and foresaw times that would be rich in God's goodness and presence once again. They foresaw a time when plants would bloom in the desert and streams of blessing would run where

FIVE SMOOTH STONES
Learning to overcome our Goliaths

there were none; where the new wine would run down from the mountains.

What the Old Testament prophets didn't fully appreciate was that before the 'day of the Lord' arrived, the Messiah would first come to inaugurate an era when judgement would be withheld and, instead, the kingdom of God would come. In place of judgement he would bring forgiveness of sin and empowerment by the Holy Spirit. This would lead to a time when men and women would have the opportunity to be cleansed and made strong, to learn to overcome and to reach out to others, to save them too from the inevitable impending judgement day.

John the Baptist announced that Jesus would baptise in spirit and in fire (Matthew 3:11). He was referring to a fire that would burn up sin and allow men and women of God to walk in holiness, rather than to the final judgement of the anticipated 'day of the Lord'. Believers could allow the Holy Spirit convict them of sin *now*, in this season of mercy, rather than wait until the day of reckoning. They could humble themselves, in response to the conviction brought by the Holy Spirit, and through repentance and faith walk free of sin. The fire that Jesus brought, then, is an expression of God's mercy rather than judgement, pending the 'day of the Lord'.

Our job in the kingdom, therefore, cannot be to exercise judgement on God's behalf (the Holy Spirit is the one who brings conviction) but is instead to demonstrate and radiate God's mercy in the world (which means in

FIVE SMOOTH STONES
Learning to overcome our Goliaths

our churches, families and marriages too). Who are we to judge when we've been let off the hook and even God doesn't judge in this season?

The final stone, therefore, to complement forgiveness, is to refrain from judging. Instead we can demonstrate the mercy of God wherever we go. If Jesus didn't come to judge we certainly aren't called to. No, we have each been forgiven much so we are to reflect his love. So that, in this season of grace, before Christ returns, we too can be instruments of salvation rather than conviction and judgement.

Jesus of course says the same thing many times in different ways: *For I did not come to judge the world but to save it* (John 12:47) and he tells us not to judge — lest we be judged! (e.g. Matthew 7:1).

We love hearing that we are no longer condemned (Romans 8:1, the climax to Paul's gospel in the book of Romans), but, perversely, we can be quick to condemn other people. It's the nature of the flesh to judge others, and we can justify it to ourselves so easily! We become blind to our own big faults as we examine the small wrongdoings in each other.

A theologian once expressed it thus, the judge was judged in our place so that we were freed from having to judge. The world is crying out for a revelation of God's mercy!

To walk without judging takes constant attention, and can seem as difficult in our natural state as walking in

**FIVE SMOOTH STONES
Learning to overcome our Goliaths**

complete forgiveness. When we are baptised and empowered by the Holy Spirit however it is not just required but demanded. It requires our willingness to identify ourselves with Christ at Calvary, to walk not in the flesh but in the Spirit. It is never what I want to do or indeed what my self-righteousness demands, but it is what God requires and gloriously enables.

Summary

All these are possible as we acknowledge our impotence in our own strength to walk in any of them

- Nothing outside a man can make him unclean — it's only your own heart that can do that — and Christ has given you a new one (Mark 7, Ezekiel 36)!

- You are no longer controlled by the flesh — your own or anybody else's (Romans 8).

- Protect your heart; only allow wisdom from God to reach your heart (James 3:13-18).

- Forgive, forgive, and forgive. Always (e.g. Matt. 6:14; Mark 11:25; Luke 23:34).

- Never judge others. Humble yourself under the mighty hand of God (e.g. Matt 7:1; Luke 6:37; 1 Peter 5:6).

All these are possible as we acknowledge our impotence in our own strength to walk in any of them.

FIVE SMOOTH STONES
Learning to overcome our Goliaths

Instead we can lean on the miracle- working power of the Holy Spirit in and through our lives. Whatever or whoever happens around us, we can walk in personal revival in our relationships. We can be all Christ asks us to be, walking in openness and vulnerability (non-defensive), displaying all the fruit of the Holy Spirit: love, joy, peace, patience, kindness, goodness, faithfulness, gentleness and self-control. This is the fruit that he bears in our lives as we walk with him! This will mean facing our Goliaths.

David's heart

God loved David's heart — not his sin (which he hated) but his heart. When we read some of the Psalms that are attributed to David perhaps we can begin to understand why. Some books in the Old Testament are history, others poetry and wisdom, but the Psalms give us a glimpse into the hearts of men who lived for God thousands of years ago.

David isn't working out his problems by talking to people, or even working things out himself, but instead realises that God alone is the one who can change things.

Three things become immediately apparent to me when I look at them. First, the authentic tone of the heart cries. Second, the hard realities of life worked through by the psalmists (as true today as then). Third, the intimate and direct nature of the psalmist–God conversation. By which I mean that David isn't working out his problems by talking to people, or even working things out himself, but instead realises that *God alone* is the one who can change things. It is God who gets the full brunt of his plea and heart cry.

FIVE SMOOTH STONES
Learning to overcome our Goliaths

Just looking at Psalms 43 and 41, for instance — by no means the most dismal! We see David is faced with slander and malice from enemies (41:5-6); attacks from those he considered friends (9); assault from deceitful and wicked men (43:1); rejection by God (2); oppression by his enemy (2b); depression (5). These are all real and potentially soul-destroying problems. David realises that it is only God who can save him, that he is truly sovereign and that he can appeal to him on that basis. He is secure enough in the knowledge of his sovereignty to be real and to know that he'll come through because of who God is, rather than to any others' intervention –least of all through anything he can do himself.

Someone once said that in times of trouble we should 'ask questions (of God), stay with God in the trauma — ask him about it, express your feelings to him and **stay connected**'. This, according to the Psalms is biblically sound.

Conclusion

Will we look to God when faced with overpowering circumstances?

As a younger man, David learned to handle confidently the sling and stones and bravely took on Goliath when no others would. Our Goliaths are the catalysts for faith or fear in our lives. Will we look to man (ourselves, others, circumstances, self-effort) or, like David, look to God when faced with overpowering circumstances? Or will we allow the things around us to drag us down into fear? Or will we look upwards at the sovereignty of God

FIVE SMOOTH STONES
Learning to overcome our Goliaths

who made all things? *Do you not know, have you not heard, I am the everlasting God!!*

Your stones will possibly be different from mine. God has been speaking to you and training you over years — and will continue to do so! What have seemed like insurmountable problems have actually been opportunities to get hold of God's word and make it real in your life; to pick stones from the stream and learn to use them. It has all been training — so that now you can be as Christ in the world. You can now advance his purposes and reveal him wherever he sends you. It's not time to rest on your laurels but, instead, to be all Christ has commissioned you to be. It has only just begun! He is God, the author and perfector of your faith.

2.

FIVE SMOOTH STONES PART TWO

STUDY GUIDE

These notes consist of four sets of questions, which, I suggest, can be used over consecutive weekly meetings. They are ideal to use in a church house-group or existing The Way of the Spirit group. Not every question has an answer that can be found in the text (though many can). All questions are designed to stimulate further thought and discussion. Be careful not to get distracted by fruitless theological intricacies or argument! The questions should not require lengthy answers.

FIVE SMOOTH STONES
Learning to overcome our Goliaths

1. First, read the relevant part of the booklet. Look up and read the Biblical passages shown.
2. Second, read the passages at the head of the questions (if different). Now referring back to the booklet as required, answer all the questions for that week.
3. Write down your answers, as briefly as possible, using only a few words, or at most a couple of sentences each time. As you do so, pray the Lord will show you how your reading and answers are to relate to your own life as a Christian.
4. If you discuss the readings in a group, try to stick to the set themes. It is so easy to go off at tangents, consider many interesting topics, and in the end miss the whole purpose of the study. The questions are to help you avoid doing that, by keeping your thoughts directed to the important, central issues.
5. If you use the CD that goes with this booklet, listen to it straight through in one sitting before you start your study; then listen to it again in parts relating to the study you are doing at the time. It contains one continuous sermon, unlike The Way of the Spirit Bible Reading Course CD's that have systematic teaching arranged in twenty-minute parts.
6. In a group, do not hurry the study. Its purpose is to help you grow spiritually as well as in understanding, and that takes prayer as well as reading.

FIVE SMOOTH STONES
Learning to overcome our Goliaths

Week ONE (Pages 7-16)

1. **Jesus speaks to the church — Revelation 2 and 3; 21:1-7**
   What do the letters to the churches have in common?

   Christ did a finished work on the cross. So what are we to overcome?

FIVE SMOOTH STONES
Learning to overcome our Goliaths

2. **Look up and see me! — Isaiah 40-41**
How does God's word compare with men's lives?

Sum up chapter 40 in your own words.

What is compared with what in chapter 41? (Compare v 7 with 8-10, for instance)

39

FIVE SMOOTH STONES
Learning to overcome our Goliaths

What does the sovereignty of God mean to you?

3. **David and Goliath — 1 Samuel 17; Luke 22:54-62; Acts 2:1-41**
Why were the Israelite soldiers afraid of Goliath?

Why did Peter deny Christ, and how did he change after Pentecost?

FIVE SMOOTH STONES
Learning to overcome our Goliaths

When do you need to overcome fear?

Describe David's attitude towards Goliath. Do you need to check your attitude?

FIVE SMOOTH STONES
Learning to overcome our Goliaths

Week TWO (Pages 16-23)

4. **Jesus and Pilate — John 18:28-19:16; Isaiah 53; Acts 7:54-60**

    See Jesus coming out in front of the crowd in John 19:5. How does he look at them? What would your attitude be towards the crowd? What is his?

    How does Stephen face a similar situation? What enables Stephen to be as Christ here?

FIVE SMOOTH STONES
Learning to overcome our Goliaths

5.   **Responses to Jesus — Mark 6:56-7:36**
Note the different responses to Jesus in this passage. How many people respond in faith, and who are they? How do the Pharisees and teachers of the law respond?

What and who can make us unclean?

What responses are there in the passage that illustrates what our new hearts are capable of?

FIVE SMOOTH STONES
Learning to overcome our Goliaths

6. **Life through the Spirit — Romans 7-8**
Chapter 7 is mainly about the law, the old covenant. What is the 'new way of the Spirit'?

Are we ever in danger of attempting to fulfil the new covenant by old covenant methods? Are you? Explain.

Chapter 8 is about life in the Spirit — the new covenant. What is affected by this covenant?

FIVE SMOOTH STONES
Learning to overcome our Goliaths

Who are you controlled by?

WEEK THREE (Pages 23-29)

7. **Who do I listen to? — James 3:13 - 4:12; Proverbs 5:1-6, 4:23**
    Who are we to listen to, and how do we recognise wisdom?

Have there been times in your life when you wish you hadn't listened to someone? Explain.

FIVE SMOOTH STONES
Learning to overcome our Goliaths

Listening for God's wisdom means being open to it from wherever it comes. How open are you?

How are we to protect our hearts?

8. **Forgiveness — Ephesians 4:32; Colossians 3:12-13; Luke 23:32-43; John 20:19-23**
   What is the first command the risen Jesus gives his disciples? What is the significance of this command?

FIVE SMOOTH STONES
Learning to overcome our Goliaths

How can we forgive people when they act so atrociously sometimes?

How do you get on with applying the command to totally forgive, as your Father has forgiven you? Is there someone now, alive or dead, who you need to forgive? Take time to pray this one through and *walk free.*

Who is most damaged when we hold on to unforgiveness? How do we help others to walk free? (Consider Stephen at his martyrdom. What enabled him?)

FIVE SMOOTH STONES
Learning to overcome our Goliaths

How are you at forgiving yourself? i.e. not allowing condemnation in your own life (See Romans 8:1)? Take time to receive his forgiveness afresh right now. *Choose to walk free.*

WEEK FOUR (Pages 29-35)

9. **The judged judge — Malachi 3.1-4; 4.1-3; Zechariah 13 7-9; Matthew 3.11-12; 7.1-5**
   What did the prophets in the Old Testament look ahead to?

FIVE SMOOTH STONES
Learning to overcome our Goliaths

How did Jesus fulfil their prophecies? What is the role of the fire, and how is it a blessing to us today?

Who does the judging — and when? Who does the convicting? What are we to do?

10. **Five Smooth Stones**
Which of the five stones described here are relevant to you? How have you been challenged?

49

FIVE SMOOTH STONES
Learning to overcome our Goliaths

Other than the ones in this study, what are the stones God has taught you to handle? Have you mastered them yet?

Do you recognise the true fight to be going on in your own heart? Do you need to let go of trying to change other people? Or are you blaming circumstances — or God even? Discuss!

What action has this study prompted?

FIVE SMOOTH STONES
Learning to overcome our Goliaths

11. God alone is your refuge! Psalms 31 and 35
   Read through slowly. List each ordeal David faced.

   List the answers he came up with.

   What might he have done instead of crying out to God?

FIVE SMOOTH STONES
Learning to overcome our Goliaths

In what wrong places are you looking for salvation from difficult circumstances?

Read Romans 8:28-39. Take courage, look up at God, and face your Goliaths. Encourage each other!

Why has God allowed certain difficult circumstances in your life?

Please now read, and if you agree, pray the declaration on the next pages.

FIVE SMOOTH STONES
Learning to overcome our Goliaths

FIVE SMOOTH STONES - a declaration

God has given me a new heart! He's taken away my heart of stone and given me a heart of flesh. Jesus died to give me this new heart! It is my fault alone if I allow it to become hardened, calloused resentful and bitter. I acknowledge that 'nothing outside a man can defile a man' and that therefore nothing anyone else says or does to me can spoil my new heart unless I allow them/it to.

I am no longer controlled by the flesh, mine or anyone else's! The Holy Spirit now controls me, so need not react or respond in any way other than how Jesus would have done. The Holy Spirit who is full of love, joy, peace, patience, kindness, gentleness, faithfulness and self-control controls me now. No one else, nor any circumstance, can make me act in any other way, if I do it's because I choose to.

I will only listen to that which is wisdom from God in my life, that is if it comes from any heart which is pure, peace- loving, considerate, submissive, full of mercy and good fruit. If it's not, but instead comes from a heart where envy and selfish ambition dwells, then I do not receive it, it is earthly, unspiritual and from the devil. I especially do not let it get anywhere near my heart. Father, forgive me for having listened to such things in the past, taking them on board and allowing them to condemn me and poison my heart. Where God has spoken to me through a good heart and I've failed

FIVE SMOOTH STONES
Learning to overcome our Goliaths

to receive it as wisdom from him, forgive me and I choose to receive it now.

I forgive all who have spoken to me with a wrong heart, and all who have hurt me in any way. If I have allowed myself to become bitter or resentful it is my fault, my responsibility alone. I do not blame them, but forgive them. In this way I release them to you for you to deal with out of your love and wisdom.

Father, forgive me where I've judged anyone else. It is not for me to judge and I repent of doing so. You did not give me a judgemental heart and I choose not to operate in judgement. You do not even judge in this season, you came to bring mercy not judgement – how dare I judge anyone else!

FIVE SMOOTH STONES
Learning to overcome our Goliaths

THE WAY OF THE SPIRIT

The Way of the Spirit has a series of Bible reading and study programmes, giving a guide to the whole Bible as seen through the activity and experience of the Holy Spirit.

HOME AND FURTHER STUDY COURSES

Six levels of study and training are available:

1. **Short Bible Reading Courses**

    • 4-6 weeks • on certain Biblical themes • for home or group study.

2. **The full length Bible Reading Course**

    • 4 six-month parts • giving complete coverage of the Bible • for home, correspondence, group, church, or college use.

3. **Biblical Commentaries**

    • 8 weeks • more detailed studies of single books of the Bible • for home or group study.

4. **Biblical and Prophetic Faith (Certificate)**

    • Two years • the full Bible course plus discipleship and ministry training • local group, class and seminar teaching.

5. **Prophetic Bible Teaching (Diploma)**

    • One year • Part-time training for local church or group Bible teaching • three short residential schools and monitored home study.

FIVE SMOOTH STONES
Learning to overcome our Goliaths

6. **Prophetic Bible Teaching (Full-Time Training)**

    • Variable duration depending on qualifications and experience • a course for training Bible teachers for more long-term works • full-time residential training.

FOR DETAILS OF ANY OF THESE COURSES, PLEASE WRITE TO:

The Way of the Spirit
Framingham Earl Hall, Framingham Earl,
Norwich, Norfolk NR14 7SB

Or visit our web site www.thewayofthespirit.com
www.facebook.com/thewayofthespirit
e-mail resources@thewayofthespirit.com
tel: 01508 495346